The Desert Photo Project started while I was living and working in Las Vegas. I spent a lot of time photographing new buildings and homes springing up in the ever-expanding suburbs of Las Vegas. One day while out in the desert in what would become a new suburb I noticed some Cacti blooming and it struck me that there is a lot of beauty in the desert, and that a lot of it is quickly disappearing. With that thought I started to record some of the things that I find interesting in the desert. I have always had a wanderlust and this idea gave me the excuse to wander even more. What follows in the book is the first few years of my explorations of the desert in no particular order. I am not a very verbal man so I will let my photographs do most of the talking, only occasionally chiming in to ad context as needed.

I do have a few thanks to some folks, Michelle who I dragged off on many occasions on long rough drives out in the desert in the middle of nowhere, (she eventually started to enjoy it) and the Nevada Back Roaders, a group of great people that really know how to enjoy the desert. I found many new and interesting places from them. Also many thanks to Matt, Levi, and Denna who also wandered off to find nothing Nowhere.

I hope you enjoy
Bob Clarke

Natural Bridge. Bryce Canyon, Utah

Bryce Canyon, Utah

Joshua Tree National Park, California

Joshua Tree National Park, California

Shoe Tree Route 66 outside of Amboy, California

Barrel Cacti. Southern, Nevada

Devil's Garden, Utah

Devil's Garden, Utah

Cholla Cacti, Southern Nevada

Teddy Bear Cacti. Southern Nevada

Teenie Weenie Little Ittsy Bitsy Flowers. Nevada

The Devil's Golf Course. Death Valley, California

Old Mule Train, Burned Cars, and a Dead Guy. You never know what you will find in the Desert.

Some times you find things in the middle of nowhere that make you ponder just a bit, hummm

The Race Track. Death Valley, California

Bad Water. Death Valley, California

Scotties Castle. Death Valley, California

Petroglyph that I believe could be a map of the valley it is in. Southern Nevada

Where there is water there is Life. Dry lake, Nevada

Cathedral Gorge State Park. Nevada

Flowers, Desert National Wildlife Refuge. Nevada

Flowers, Desert National Wildlife Refuge. Nevada

Flowers, Desert National Wildlife Refuge. Nevada

Nellis Dunes just north of Las Vegas. A great place to play with the **4X4**. Nevada

Yucca Blum. Nevada

Desert National Wildlife Refuge. Nevada

Elephant Rock, Valley of Fire State Park. Nevada

Red Rock Canyon. Nevada

Boiler for an old Steam Engine. Mt. Charleston. Nevada

Flowers

Paintings by Roy Purcell. Chloride, Arizona

Chloride, Arizona

Nelson, Nevada

Buck Canyon
Overlook 200 Ft

No
Camping

They are watching me.

I am often followed in my travels; I am not sure what to make of this?

CanyonLands National Park, Utah

CanyonLands National Park, Utah

Along the Colorado River, Utah

Wupatki National Monument, Arizona

Keyhole Canyon, Nevada

What can I say; You can drive to "B.F.E." in Utah.

Capitol Reef National Park, Utah

Kinda sorta near Pahrump, Nevada

"The Ditch" - Grand Canyon National Park, Arizona

Chaco Culture National Historical Park, New Mexico

Arches National Park, Utah

Prickly Pear Cacti near Lake Mead, Nevada

Bang bang, he shot me down Bang bang, I hit the ground
Bang bang, that awful sound Bang bang, my baby shot me down.

Red Rock Canyon, Nevada

Help! Help! The Bush Sprung a leek!

Near Moab, Utah

Dry Lake near, Las Vegas, Nevada

Valley of Fire State Park, Nevada

Zion National Park, Utah

Zion National Park, Utah

Zion National Park, Utah

Pipe Springs National Monument, Arazona

www.ingramcontent.com/pod-product-compliance
Lightning Source LLC
Chambersburg PA
CBHW041509280526
45792CB00004B/1189